Garfield County Libraries
Silt Branch Library
680 Home Avenue
Silt, CO 81652
(970) 876-5500 • Fax (970) 876-5921
www.GCPLD.org

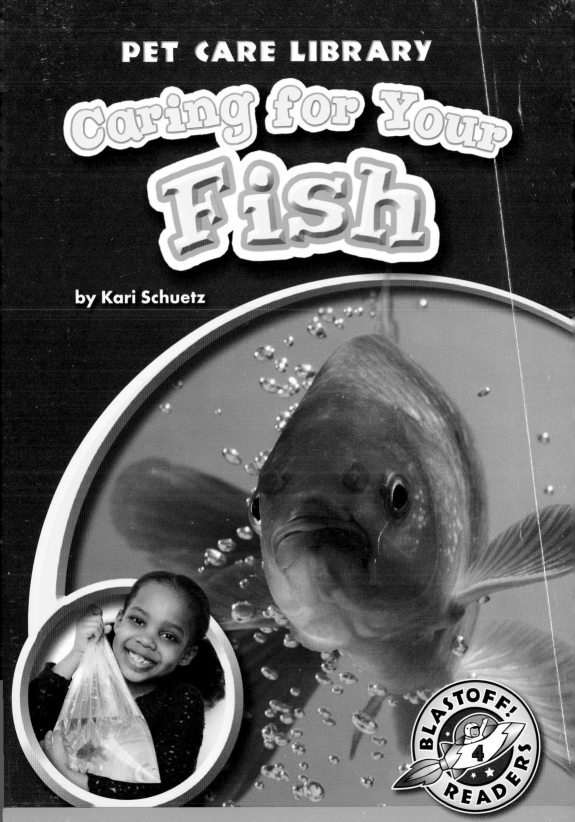

PET CARE LIBRARY

Caring for Your Fish

by Kari Schuetz

BELLWETHER MEDIA · MINNEAPOLIS, MN

BLASTOFF!
READERS
4

Note to Librarians, Teachers, and Parents:

Blastoff! Readers are carefully developed by literacy experts and combine standards-based content with developmentally appropriate text.

Level 1 provides the most support through repetition of high-frequency words, light text, predictable sentence patterns, and strong visual support.

Level 2 offers early readers a bit more challenge through varied simple sentences, increased text load, and less repetition of high-frequency words.

Level 3 advances early-fluent readers toward fluency through increased text and concept load, less reliance on visuals, longer sentences, and more literary language.

Level 4 builds reading stamina by providing more text per page, increased use of punctuation, greater variation in sentence patterns, and increasingly challenging vocabulary.

Level 5 encourages children to move from "learning to read" to "reading to learn" by providing even more text, varied writing styles, and less familiar topics.

Whichever book is right for your reader, Blastoff! Readers are the perfect books to build confidence and encourage a love of reading that will last a lifetime!

This edition first published in 2011 by Bellwether Media, Inc.

No part of this publication may be reproduced in whole or in part without written permission of the publisher. For information regarding permission, write to Bellwether Media, Inc., Attention: Permissions Department, 5357 Penn Avenue South, Minneapolis, MN 55419.

Library of Congress Cataloging-in-Publication Data
Schuetz, Kari.
Caring for your fish / by Kari Schuetz.
  p. cm. – (Blastoff! readers. Pet care library)
Summary: "Developed by literacy experts for students in grades two through five, this title provides readers with basic information for taking care of fish"–Provided by publisher.
 Includes bibliographical references and index.
ISBN 978-1-60014-467-7 (hardcover : alk. paper)
1. Aquarium fishes–Juvenile literature. 2. Aquariums–Juvenile literature. I. Title.
SF457.25.S26 2010
639.34–dc22   2010011488

Printed in the United States of America, North Mankato, MN.
080110   1162

Contents

Choosing a Fish

Fish are popular **aquatic** pets. Many people enjoy taking care of them and watching them swim.

Fish come in many colorful varieties. Some live in freshwater while others live in saltwater.

! fun fact

You will never see a fish close its eyes or blink. Fish do not have eyelids!

guppy

betta fish

goldfish

Learn about different kinds of fish before you choose your pet. If you want more than one fish, be sure to pick kinds of fish that get along. Some fish attack or even try to eat other fish.

Make sure you are ready to care for a pet fish.
A fish requires your attention every day to stay
happy and healthy. Many species of fish can live
for 10 to 20 years.

Setting Up a Fish Tank

Your fish will need an underwater home. Choose a large tank instead of a small bowl. A large tank gives fish more room to swim. It also allows you more control over the **water quality**.

Pick a special place for the tank. Keep it away from windows and doors. Sunlight or cool air can cause the **water temperature** in the tank to change. Once you've selected a spot for the tank, go to a pet store to get the supplies you will need to properly care for your fish.

Supply List

Here is a list of supplies you will need to take care of a fish.

- tank with cover
- plants
- gravel
- filter
- heater
- thermometer
- fish food
- small net

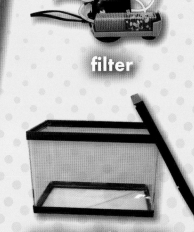

filter

tank with cover

small net

filter

gravel

You can decorate the tank with **gravel** and plants. Gravel gives waste a place to settle. The plants give your fish hiding places that make them feel safe.

heater with thermometer

! fun fact

Fish are cold-blooded animals. Their bodies are the temperature of the water around them.

Connect a **filter** to the tank to remove harmful chemicals and waste from the water. Also attach a heater and a **thermometer** to maintain and monitor the water temperature in the tank.

It is best to put a cover on the tank. This will prevent objects from falling into the tank and your fish from jumping out. It will also keep the water from **evaporating**.

About a week before you bring your fish home, fill the tank with clean **tap water**. Let the water **age**. It takes time for the water to become safe for your fish.

Bringing Your Fish Home

Visit a pet store to buy your fish. Choose from among **hardy** varieties like goldfish and guppies. It is best to start with one or two fish.

Bring your fish home in a plastic bag full of water. Before you release your fish into its tank, float the bag in the tank for at least 30 minutes. You need to wait for the water temperatures in the tank and bag to match.

Care Tip

Fish are very sensitive to changes in temperature. A large, quick change can harm or kill a fish.

Feeding Your Fish

Most fish eat two small
meals each day. Every morning
and evening, drop a few flakes or
one pellet into the tank. Watch your
hungry fish swim to the surface and eat.

Be careful not to overfeed your fish. Uneaten food will spoil in the tank and **pollute** the water. Polluted water can make your fish sick.

🐟 Care Tip

A healthy fish needs variety in its diet. Once a week, treat your fish to brine shrimp, bloodworms, tubifex worms, or lettuce leaves.

Keeping Your Fish Healthy

Care Tip

Always move your fish with a small net. If you touch your fish, you can harm its gills or remove the slime that protects its body.

algae

Sick fish often lose their color or develop spots. Most hide and barely move. If you have a sick fish, put it in another tank. Ask a pet care expert how to care for it.

Prevent sickness by keeping the tank clean. Every few weeks, remove some of the **algae** that has grown in the tank. Replace some of the tank water with clean, aged tap water.

Training Your Fish

Fish are smarter than many people think. You can train your fish to follow your finger or eat from your hand. You might even notice your fish swim toward you when you are near the tank.

You can also try to teach your fish fun tricks. With practice and treats, many fish can learn to swim through obstacles and even fetch objects!

! fun fact

A goldfish named Comet holds the Guinness World Record for "World's Smartest Fish." Comet performed nine tricks to earn the title!

Glossary

age—to sit for a period of time; water needs to age before it is safe for pet fish.

algae—plantlike organisms that live in water

aquatic—living in water

evaporating—changing from a liquid to a gas

filter—a device that water passes through; a filter removes chemicals and waste from water.

gravel—small pieces of rock

hardy—strong and able to survive harsh or changing conditions

pollute—to make dirty

tap water—water that comes from a faucet

thermometer—an instrument that measures temperature

water quality—how clean the water is; healthy fish need clean water.

water temperature—how hot or cold the water is

To Learn More

AT THE LIBRARY

Bozzo, Linda. *My First Fish*. Berkeley Heights, N.J.: Enslow, 2008.

Stevens, Kathryn. *Fish*. Mankato, Minn.: The Child's World, 2009.

Wood, Selina. *Fish*. North Mankato, Minn.: Sea to Sea Publications, 2007.

ON THE WEB

Learning more about pet care is as easy as 1, 2, 3.

1. Go to www.factsurfer.com.

2. Enter "pet care" into the search box.

3. Click the "Surf" button and you will see a list of related Web sites.

With factsurfer.com, finding more information is just a click away.

Index